# Ten Key Promises from the Bible

by Karen Locken

**Bible Basics for Adults**

Augsburg Fortress, Minneapolis

# Contents

**BIBLE BASICS FOR ADULTS**
*Ten Key Promises from the Bible* Learner Book
This learner book has a corresponding leader guide.

Editors: Katherine A. Evensen, Eric P. Vollen, and Doug Schmitz
Designer: Craig P. Claeys. Illustrators: Mari Goering and Judy Swanson

From the writer and editors: It is our greatest hope that as you study God's promises, you will be able to identify how those promises include you. May God's peace and grace be with you as you study!

Note of thanks: I am incredibly grateful for the help of my husband, Rev. Douglas Locken, who has assisted with the research for this project. —Karen Locken

Scripture quotations are from New Revised Standard Version Bible, copyright 1989 Division of Christian Education of the National Council of the Churches of Christ in the United States of America. Used by permission.

ISBN 0-8066-3636-X

Manufactured in U.S.A.
1 2 3 4 5 6 7 8 9 0 1 2 3 4 5 6 7 8 9

# ① God Promises a Future

In spite of human sin, God promises continued life for generations to come.

## Genesis 8:20-22  God's Promise to Noah

*After the Ark: The Rest of Noah's Story*

A FTER SPENDING A YEAR ON THE ARK, I, Noah, was thrilled to set foot on dry ground. My wife and I first danced for joy, then set about giving thanks to God for getting us through this amazing high water adventure.

After all, it had been incredible. For 40 days and nights it poured rain. And I mean it poured. Of course, there has never been anything like it and never will be again. My boat floated high above the earth's mountain tops. After it finally stopped raining, it took a long time for the water to give way to dry land. Those days of waiting were hard. Ark fever—which could be likened to cabin fever—set in and there was little one could do to avoid it. During the day, we kept busy caring for the animals, but the nights were long. Minutes felt like hours. Sometimes I wondered if this mission would ever end. I wondered whether I

would ever again be able to stretch out under the shade of a tall cypress and snooze on a bed of soft green grass. I wondered if I would ever again see the colorful burst of wildflowers in bloom. I wondered whether I would ever again taste the sun sweetened fruit of God's good earth. How I longed to sink my teeth into a ripened red tomato and feel the juice drip down my chin. In my darkest moments, I feared that my life would end in the dark of the damp, smelly ark. But then I would remember that it had been God who started me on this journey and I knew, somewhere in the deep of my being, that God would get me through it.

After all, God had not left me alone. Not only was I surrounded by every breathing beast of the earth, God had blessed me with family. Although our quarters closed in on us at times and occasionally we touched on one another's nerves, my wife, along with our three sons Shem, Ham, and Japheth, and their wives helped me realize that being a part of a family—being connected in community—is one of God's greatest blessings. Our family was the beginning of the earth's population.

> **The dove,** often a symbol of the Holy Spirit, is a sign of new life.

As sure as the world turns, as long as I live, I will never forget the day the dove came back with a freshly plucked leaf from an olive tree. The hope, the fulfillment of promise, the faith that was symbolized by that one leaf makes my heart flutter to this day.

A few days later when God called us forth from the ark, we could have kissed the ground. I was so happy I built an altar and made an offering to God. I wanted to give back a portion of what God had given me. God, wholly pleased by the offering, made an incredible promise to me and my family that will affect every generation to come. God promised in spite of human sin, never again would the creation be destroyed. God promised from this day forward, "As long as the earth endures, seedtime and harvest, cold and heat, summer and winter, day and night, shall not cease" (Genesis 8:22). In that promise, my own future and the future of humankind was changed forever.

> **Noah's altar** was the first altar ever built. The building of altars continued to be a practice when the Israelites experienced the presence of God.

*Sometimes Life Is Funny*

I PROBABLY SHOULD NOT HAVE LAUGHED, but it was funny. Me, Abraham, formerly known as Abram, and my wife Sarah, formerly known as Sarai, in our old age were promised a son. I thought God had an incredible sense of humor. But, it seems, God was not joking. God was serious. Although I was 100 years old, and although my wife was 90, God announced that we were going to have a baby—a son named Isaac.

I should have known about God's promises. After all, God and I had a long standing relationship that started way back with my ancestor Noah. I, of course, am a descendant of Noah through the lineage of his son, Shem.

Earlier in my life, after I had moved to Haran with my father, Terah; my wife, Sarai; and my nephew, Lot; God told me to leave my homeland and go to a new place where my descendants would become a great nation. I did as I was told. The Lord had always kept the promises that were made to my family.

To say the least, it was an adventure. When I got to a place called Shechem in the land of the Canaanites, God promised to give that land to my offspring. I built an altar there to worship God. We continued our journey living out of a tent.

God refers to Abraham's offspring seven times before the promise is fulfilled. (See Genesis 12:2, 12:7, 13:14-16, 15:5, 17:2-8, 17:16-19, and 18:14.)

Those years were difficult for Sarai and me. Wandering through the desert, living out of a tent, moving from place to place, was not an easy life. It got more difficult when a famine hit. Sarai and I had to go to Egypt.

Yet, as I think about it, God has always provided for me and kept the promises that have been made. But the promise of offspring made me wonder. So many times God has told me that my descendants would be many and would even become a great nation. But yet, Sarai and I had never conceived a child. It is not that we had not tried. We even went so far as to use Hagar as a surrogate

© 1998 Richard Nowitz

mother (see Genesis 16). Although I love my son, Ishmael, that surrogate business brought its own set of troubles. I guess we just had a hard time waiting. We grew impatient. We thought we needed to take things into our own hands.

In spite of it all, here was God's voice again telling me that the promise would come true. Not only did God rename my wife and me thereby claiming us as God's own, but God went so far as to name the son that is to come. His name will be Isaac. Funny thing, the name *Isaac* means "he laughs."

Though it literally took a lifetime for God's promises to finally be fulfilled for Sarah and me, one thing I realized was that God always does fulfill the promises God makes. Sometimes it does seem to take a long time, but God is faithful. No matter who you are, no matter how strange the journey, God always comes through.

# Focus the Stories

*Promises, Promises*

THE STORIES OF GOD'S PROMISES to Noah and Abraham remind us that God is always faithful in keeping promises despite human sin. Our experience with human promises is not always that way. How do God's promises differ from human promises?

Read the following vignettes; then write a few notes in response to the questions that follow.

Jack (age 48): "My boss promised that my company's merger would not affect my position, but they eliminated my job within three months. Now I have no income, no health insurance, no benefits. What a fool I was to believe her."

Tyler (age 10): "My Dad promised that even though he and Mom were getting divorced and he was moving out of our house, that we would still see him every other weekend. But, he has a girlfriend now. Her name is Lisa. She does not like kids. I have not seen my Dad in three months. What a dope I was to believe him."

Amber (age 19): "He said he loved me. He said he would always love me. He said he had never been with anyone else before. I trusted him. Now I am seven-months pregnant. I have not seen him since I told him five months ago. Worse yet, I just found out that I am HIV-positive. My baby might be infected too. What a fool I was to believe him."

*Questions*

*1.* What experiences have you had with promises in your life?

*2.* Have you or anyone you know experienced situations similar to Jack's, Tyler's, or Amber's?

God's promises to Noah and Abraham tell us that God's promises operate differently than human promises. Consider the following questions:

*3.* What promises has God made to you?

*4.* What has been your experience with God's promises?

*5.* What would you tell Jack, Tyler, or Amber about God's promises?

# ② God Promises Unending Protection

Throughout life's trials and temptations,
God continues to provide protection.

## Psalm 121 God: The Keeper of Life

THE WORD *KEEPER* CONJURES UP IMAGES of housekeepers and gardeners. Housekeepers are people whose job it is to make sure a house is properly cleaned. They remove dust, scrub away germs, sweep up the dirt, and leave a home looking and smelling its absolute best. Gardeners are people who tend growing plants. They remove the weeds, provide water and other nutrients for optimal plant productivity, prune branches that hinder growth, and leave a piece of landscape that is not only

beautifully pleasing to the eye, but a source of life for other earthly inhabitants. Clearly, the role of a housekeeper and gardener is that of a servant. Although rarely the invited guest of an affluent party host, the party would not be possible without the unseen presence of the servant.

In Psalm 121, God is identified as a "keeper." Like the housekeeper and the gardener, God's role of keeper is that of a servant.

The psalmist identifies God as the keeper who never sleeps, the keeper who will guard against evil, the keeper of life from this time on and forevermore. This is an incredible glimpse of God. The God revealed in this psalm is not only a God of promise, but a God who intimately connects with every aspect of daily life.

Psalm 121 is generally understood as a conversation between two people. The psalmist assures the question seeker (verse 1) of two extremely important aspects of God. The first is that God continues moment by moment, day by day, year by year, century after century to interact with creation. Creating the world was not a one-time event, but is a continual process in which God is always and forever the architect.

Skjold Photographs

The second aspect the psalmist identifies is that God is a God of unending love. Like a parent who cannot sleep until the teenage child is safely home, like the neighbor who carefully notices the comings and goings of the elderly woman next door, like the teacher whose eyes rove the playground for signs of trouble, God is watching out, keeping track, ultimately caring for humankind every moment of every hour of every day.

Proclaiming the trustworthiness of God, the psalmist assures that "the sun shall not strike you by day or the moon by night" (verse 6). A common understanding at the time the psalmist wrote was that the moon was the cause of diseases. The reference to the sun would speak of the concern for sunstroke for those wandering in the desert. The psalmist is adamant that regardless of life's circumstances, one is always, without doubt, within the realm of God's care and deep concern.

God's promise to us is that God will always take care of us, like a devoted gardener to her garden. But more, God promises to love us and protect us "from this time on and forevermore."

# Isaiah 43:1-4  God: The Protector of Life

THIS ISAIAH TEXT is woven with promise. The prophet speaks God's word of hope to the people of Israel who are exiled in Babylon. He speaks of the depth of God's faithfulness to Israel in the past, God's partnership with Israel in the present—even in the midst of their exile—and God's promise to continue living in relationship with the people of Israel in the future.

The first verse refers to God's relationship with Jacob, the father of the nation Israel, (Genesis 35:10-12) where God renamed Jacob "Israel" and promised that his offspring would be a

> **Israel** was the name God gave to Jacob when he promised to make of him a great nation.

great nation. Jacob had a sordid past, so God's renaming Jacob "Israel" and renewing a shared vision for their future provided Jacob with a fresh start. But even a fresh start does not guarantee an unblemished future.

After a time, Israel again proved to be unfaithful, which resulted in their exile to Babylon. Yet God sent a prophet to the beloved people of Israel to remind them that even in the midst of their rebellion, in the midst of their frustration, in the midst of their pain, God continued to stand by them. "Do not fear, for I have redeemed you; I have called you by name, you are mine" (Isaiah 43:1b) are intimate words proclaiming the depth of God's compassion and commitment to the people of Israel. Like a parent

who longs to hold and comfort the wayward child, God sends Isaiah to proclaim God's unrelenting, unconditional love for Israel in spite of Israel's unfaithfulness.

As God's words roll off the prophet's tongue, future promise is revealed. That is, God has announced the measures that God will take to restore and protect Israel. The prophet speaks God's promise through the language of history known to the Israelites. They would remember that when God wanted their earlier prophet, Moses, to lead the Israelites out of slavery in Egypt, God got his initial attention by having flames burst forth from a bush but that the bush did not burn up (Exodus 3:2). They would also remember that when Moses first led the Israelites out of slavery in Egypt, God assisted their escape by parting the waters of the Red Sea to form a path where they were able to walk through on dry land (Exodus 14:29). By being reminded of their past, Israel can hear the fullness of God's hope for their future.

Image © 1996 PhotoDisc, Inc.

In verse 4, the depth of God's relationship with Israel is revealed: "You are precious in my sight, and honored, and I love you" (Isaiah 43:4). How many lovers can forgive unfaithful acts of their beloved again and again, yet continue to love openly and unconditionally? Like a marriage partner at the altar, God has promised again and again to be wholly present through the thick and thin of Israel's life.

And God makes the same promise to us that was made to Israel. Though we have questions and doubts and even turn away from God at times, God assures us that God will never turn away from us. God's promise to us is that we are precious and we will never be left alone—and God never breaks a promise.

# Focus the Stories

PSALM 121 AND ISAIAH 43:1-4 identify God as a protector and keeper of human life. How might we understand God as a keeper and protector of our lives? How do we understand the concepts of keeping and protecting in human relationships? Read the following story and write a few notes in response to the questions that follow.

*Jim's Story*

On our wedding day, she promised to honor and keep me until death parted us. She promised that by forsaking all others she would keep herself only unto me for the rest of our lives. I thought "to honor and keep" meant that she would love me and care for me always. I thought when she promised "to keep herself only unto me" that she would be faithful in the relationship we had with each other. I never dreamed she would ever find someone else. Growing up, I understood marriage as a protected relationship between two people. Although I knew marriages were not necessarily perfect, I believed that when people were married they tried to work out whatever problems came along. My wife started having an affair with a coworker. For a long time, I did not know. Then for awhile I refused to believe it could be true. My wife blames me for the affair. She said that I had gotten too fat, too gray, and too old. She said that I was not fun anymore. I suppose she might be right. But yet, doesn't being faithful mean that in spite of those things, we are to love and care for one another?

*Questions*

*1.* What do the words *keep* and *protect* mean to you?

*2.* How is God faithful in ways that Jim's wife was not?


*3.* Look again at Psalm 121:7-8 and Isaiah 43:1. Does God put conditions on remaining faithful?


*4.* What might you tell Jim about God's hopes for his life? For his wife's life?


*5.* Is Jim obliged to forgive as God forgives? Why or why not?

# ③ God Promises a Leader

Through prophetic voices, God identifies
a coming leader for Israel.

## Isaiah 53:1-6  The Suffering Servant

WHEN ONE READS THIS TEXT with Christian eyes, one is tempted to see this text as simply revealing the purpose and mission of Jesus Christ in saving the world. However, at the time the prophet spoke these words to the people of Israel, they did not know about Jesus. What they did know is that they had spent a long time suffering at the hands of the Babylonians. What they did know is that God had just

© 1998 Richard Nowitz

brought an end to their exile and they would be returning to Jerusalem. What they did know is that God had selected them to be God's very own people and throughout their history had demonstrated again and again that God would always be faithful to the promises God made.

Clearly, this is a pivotal time in Israel's history. Israel has been freed from captivity and is faced with a future filled with new hope and possibility.

Because of that freedom, the prophet's role has changed. Isaiah's job has now become one of providing reflection and perspective in this time of transition. Isaiah begins by reminding the people where they have been and from whom they have come. He acknowledges that suffering has been part of Israel's experience as a people. Yet, he provides the perspective that suffering is not done apart from God nor is it necessarily God's desired outcome. Isaiah proclaims that because of the intimate relationship God has with God's people, God suffers too. As one cannot remain immune to the suffering of a family member afflicted with disease, depression, unemployment, poverty, oppression, and so forth, God cannot remain apart from the suffering of God's people.

In proclaiming such truth, Isaiah's words also tell of the coming of Jesus, God's Son, who will once and for all time bear the suffering of the whole human race.

The promise of God revealed in this text is not that suffering will never occur to those claimed as God's people; but rather, that God will always, absolutely without a doubt, be present with them in their suffering.

Through the perspective of Christian understanding, the promise revealed in this text goes one step further. That is, not only is God present with us in our suffering, but through Jesus Christ, God has suffered for us.

SOMETIMES PROPHETS are sent from God with a message of judgment. Sometimes they are sent with a message of hope and compassion. Sometimes they are sent to deal with a certain social or political issue. Always they are sent by God to affect change.

Micah was a prophet who lived and worked at the same time as the prophets Isaiah, Amos, and Hosea. Like them, he spoke out against injustice and the need to turn away from evil and false worship. What Micah is most often known for, however, was his vision of the coming Messiah proclaimed in this text.

For Israel, Micah's words of the coming Messiah brought a sense of hope that was passed on from generation to generation. Even though it was centuries before the fullness of that hope was realized in the birth of Jesus, Micah's announcement of God's promise of a Messiah meant that God had not abandoned the people of Israel.

For Israel, it was a promise within a promise. That is, not only was there hope in hearing that there would be a future ruler from Bethlehem that would establish peace, there was hope in the present because in making the promise, God had entered into the depth of their experience in the here and now. For Israel, the here and now was exile in Babylon.

*(Continued on page 27)*

# HOW THE BIBLE IS ORGANIZED

The Bible is divided into two "testaments." The Old Testament, which was originally written in Hebrew, contains four major sections that include 39 individual books. The New Testament, which was originally written in Greek, is divided into three sections that include 27 books.

## THE OLD TESTAMENT

### The Pentateuch
Genesis
Exodus
Leviticus
Numbers
Deuteronomy

### History
Joshua
Judges
Ruth
1 and 2 Samuel
1 and 2 Kings
1 and 2 Chronicles
Ezra
Nehemiah
Esther

### Wisdom
Job
Psalms
Proverbs

Ecclesiastes
Song of Solomon

### Prophets
Isaiah
Jeremiah
Lamentations
Ezekiel
Daniel
Hosea
Joel
Amos
Obadiah
Jonah
Micah
Nahum
Habakkuk
Zephaniah
Haggai
Zechariah
Malachi

## THE NEW TESTAMENT

### The Gospels
Matthew
Mark
Luke
John

### History
Acts of the Apostles

### The Letters
Romans
1 and 2 Corinthians
Galatians
Ephesians

Philippians
Colossians
1 and 2 Thessalonians
1 and 2 Timothy
Titus
Philemon
Hebrews
James
1 and 2 Peter
1, 2, and 3 John
Jude
Revelation

Adapted from *A Beginner's Guide to Reading the Bible* by Craig R. Koester, copyright © 1991 Augsburg Fortress.

# BIBLE TIME LINE

| Date | Bible Story/Message | Text |
|------|---------------------|------|
| | Creation | Genesis 1:1—2:4a |
| | The Fall | Genesis 3:1-24 |
| | The Flood | Gen. 6:11-22; 9:8-17 |
| | Call of Abraham | Genesis 12:1-3 |
| | Abraham and Sarah | Genesis 18:1-15 |
| | Moses | Exodus 3:1-15 |
| 1275-1235 B.C. | Exodus and Wilderness Wandering | |
| | Wilderness Wandering | Exodus 16:1-12 |
| | The Ten Commandments | Exodus 20:1-17 |
| | The Shema | Deuteronomy 6:4-9 |
| 1200-1050 B.C. | Judges | |
| | Deborah and Barak | Judges 4:1-24 |
| | Ruth and Naomi | Ruth 1:1-18 |
| 1050-922 B.C. | United Monarchy | |
| | David | 2 Samuel 7:1-29 |
| | The Divine Shepherd | Psalm 23:1-6 |
| | Thanks for Healing | Psalm 30:4-5 |
| 922-721 B.C. | Divided Monarchy | |
| | Micah | Micah 6:8 |
| | Jeremiah | Jeremiah 1:4-19 |
| | The Fiery Furnace | Daniel 3:1-30 |
| | Fall of Northern Kingdom | 2 Kings 17:5-23 |
| 586-538 B.C. | Judah in Exile | |
| 538-333 B.C. | Persian Period | |
| 333-165 B.C. | Hellenistic Period | |
| 165-63 B.C. | Maccabean Period | |
| 63 B.C.-A.D. 637 | Roman Period | |
| | Mary | Luke 1:26-38 |

| Date | Bible Story/Message | Text |
|------|---------------------|------|
| 4 B.C. | Jesus is Born | |
| | Birth of Jesus | Luke 2:1-20 |
| | Birth of Jesus | Matthew 1:1, 17-25 |
| | Baptism of Jesus | Matthew 3:13-17 |
| | Temptation of Jesus | Luke 4:1-13 |
| A.D. 20 | Ministry of Jesus | |
| | Sermon on the Mount | Matthew 7:1-12 |
| | Healing a Paralytic | Mark 2:1-12 |
| | The Gospel in Miniature | John 3:16 |
| | Cleansing the Temple | Mark 11:15-19 |
| | Mary and Martha | Luke 10:38-42 |
| | Peter | Matthew 16:13-23 |
| | The Lord's Supper | Matthew 26:17-30 |
| | I Am the Way | John 14:6 |
| | The Crucifixion | Mark 15:21-39 |
| | The Death of Jesus | John 19:1-30 |
| | The Road to Emmaus | Luke 24:13-35 |
| | Jesus' Resurrection | John 20:1-18 |
| | The Ascension of Jesus | Acts 1:6-11 |
| | Pentecost | Acts 2:1-14, 37-42 |
| A.D. 40 | Apostles' Ministry | |
| | Paul | Acts 9:1-22 |
| | Benediction | 2 Thess. 2:16-17 |
| | A New Creation | 2 Cor. 5:17-21 |
| | God's Love in Christ Jesus | Romans 8:31-39 |
| | By Grace | Ephesians 2:8-10 |
| | Faith | Hebrews 11:1-3 |
| | Encouragement and Warnings | Hebrews 12:1-2 |
| | The Alpha and Omega | Revelation 1:8 |

# HOW TO READ THE BIBLE

## Finding a Bible Reference

1. Check the Bible's table of contents if you do not know where the book is.
2. In your Bible, the chapter numbers are large numbers, usually at the beginning of paragraphs. The chapter numbers might be also printed at the top of each page.
3. The verse numbers are tiny numbers, usually printed at the beginning of sentences.

> ## Psalm 119:105
> book of     chapter     verse
> the Bible

## Understanding What You Read

As you read a passage of the Bible, keep in mind these three questions:
1. What does this text tell me about God?
2. What does this text tell me about the people of God?
3. What does this text tell me about myself?

## Going Deeper

Other questions that might help you understand what you are reading include:
1. What type of literature is this passage? Is it a story? A historical account? Poetry? A hymn? A letter? How might that affect my understanding of the passage?
2. What is the historical situation of the writer?
3. Who is speaking in this passage?
4. Who is being addressed in this passage? How am I like or different from that person or group?
5. How does the passage relate to the surrounding text? Does the surrounding material shed any light on the passage's meaning?
6. What are the key words and phrases in the passage? Which ones do I not understand?
7. How does the passage compare to parallel passages or to texts on the same subject?
8. What in the passage puzzles, surprises, or confuses me?

## Marking Your Bible

When you read the Bible, make notes to yourself about questions and insights you have as you read. The following symbols might be helpful.

| | |
|---|---|
| **㉓** | The circled number marks an important chapter. |
| **?** | I do not understand this. |
| **♥** | God's love is revealed in this passage. |
| **P** | One of God's promises is given here. |
| **†** | This is about something God has done for me. |
| **HS** | The work of the Holy Spirit is described here. |
| **F** | Faith, confidence, trust |
| **H** | Hope, perseverance, patience |
| **↔** | Love, relationships, social concerns |
| **✍** | Prayer |
| **♪** | Praise, joy, hymns |
| **℞** | Strength, comfort, healing |

"Going Deeper" and "Marking Your Bible" are adapted from *Bible Reading Handbook* by Paul Schuessler, copyright © 1991 Augsburg Fortress.

The people of Israel had a long history with God and therefore knew that they could rely on God's promises. Micah's reference to the leader that would come from Bethlehem, "whose origin is from of old, from ancient days"

**Bethlehem** was the birthplace of Joseph, who was engaged to Mary, the mother of Jesus.

(5:2), reminded them of more pleasant times under the rule of King David and hinted at a future when their nation would again be strong and secure.

Through the lens of Christianity, one can see more clearly the richness of this promise as it is referenced in the New Testament (Matthew 2:6). Centuries after the Babylonian exile, years and years after Micah's prophetic words were spoken, the Wise Men from the East came following the star, looking for the "king of the Jews" (Matthew 2:2). King Herod, the ruler at the time, became frightened. He was threatened by the announcement. He called together the Jewish leaders and asked them for more information. The lead-

© 1998 Richard Nowitz

ers quoted Micah saying that the Messiah was to be born in Bethlehem of Judea. King Herod in his fear sent a search party to seek out the baby King and destroy him. God, however, was again faithful to the promise made so long ago. God sent an angel to warn Joseph and Mary about King Herod. They were told to go to Egypt where they would be safe. So Joseph and Mary took baby Jesus, the long awaited King, to seek refuge in Egypt.

It was centuries of waiting before Jesus Christ finally appeared. But God did keep the promise to God's people. And like all of God's promises, the promise Micah spoke proclaimed God's ongoing commitment to the people God created. It was, and continues to be, a message a hope.

# Focus the Stories

THROUGH THE PROPHETIC VOICES of Isaiah and Micah, we have learned a number of things including: (1) suffering is a part of the human experience; (2) God will be present throughout life including times of suffering; and (3) God will send a ruler/servant that will bring a new reality to the world. As we consider the concept of suffering within the realm of God's promise, how do we understand suffering? Is all human suffering the same? Why or why not? Read the following vignettes, then reflect on the questions that follow.

David (age 51): "I don't understand why my father had such a debilitating stroke. He has been a good, faithful man all his life. He has served on the church council, been the head usher for over 25 years, and tithed to the church. So why is my father suffering?"

Kathy (age 43): "He always says he'll never do it again. Yet time and again, my husband hits me when things don't go his way. Last time we had a fight, I spent three days in the hospital with terrible bruises and two broken ribs—all because his bowling shirt wasn't clean that day. They tell me I should leave him, but when I married him, I promised for better or for worse."

Sam (age 19): "I never thought it could happen to me. We were just driving around drinking a few beers. I guess we had a few too many. We weren't paying close enough attention. We were going way too fast when we hit the curve on Highway 41. It was too late. Jay lost control of the car and we crashed into the light pole. Now Jay is paralyzed from the neck down, and they say that I may never walk again."

*Questions*

**1.** How is each person's suffering the same? How is it different?

**2.** Do some kinds of suffering go beyond the role of servant-hood? Why or why not?

**3.** What would you say about God's promises to David, Kathy, or Sam?

**4.** How are Isaiah's and Micah's messages of God's promise still important for us today? How do the prophets' messages of hope speak to you ?

# ④ God Promises Jesus the Christ

*In Jesus Christ, God gives life in the fullest sense of what it means to live.*

## Luke 1:46-55  Filled with Hope: Mary's Song

I COULD NOT WAIT to tell Elizabeth. Imagine me, Mary, the mother of God's child. When the angel told me, I could barely believe what I was hearing. After all, I am nobody special. I am not a princess or a queen. I have not done anything to earn such a privilege. Yet, God chose me.

I could hardly wait to tell Elizabeth. She knew so much about God and the promises God had made. I knew she would understand and share my great joy.

I have to admit, it was kind of scary. I was excited, but I was also scared, because being pregnant with God's child would be challenging. After all, I was a mere teenager. Besides that, I was engaged and not so sure that my fiancé, Joseph, would understand. The angel assured me that I had nothing to fear.

Elizabeth is one of those family members that you are proud to claim on your family tree. She is a wise, beautiful woman married to Zechariah, a priest. She and Zechariah have never had children although they had been married for years and have wanted to have a child for a long, long time. I remember that distant look in Elizabeth's eyes every time our family gathered to celebrate the arrival of a new baby. Actually, Elizabeth was old enough to be my grandmother or even my great-grandmother, yet we were really close. She had taught me so much about life and the God who had created us.

In some ways, this story is kind of ironic. Elizabeth was five months pregnant when I went to tell her that God had chosen me to bear a child. There we were—an old woman pregnant with her first child—and me, a teenager not yet married, pregnant with mine. In that moment when we gazed knowingly at one another—our eyes brimming with

*My soul magnifies the Lord,*
*and my spirit rejoices in God*
*my Savior,*
*for he has looked with favor on*
*the lowliness of his servant.*
*Surely, from now on all*
*generations will call me*
*blessed;*
*for the Mighty One has done*
*great things for me,*
*and holy is his name.*
*His mercy is for those who fear*
*him*
*from generation to*
*generation.*
*He has shown strength with his*
*arm;*
*he has scattered the proud in*
*the thoughts of their*
*hearts.*
*He has brought down the*
*powerful from their*
*thrones,*
*and lifted up the lowly;*
*he has filled the hungry with*
*good things,*
*and sent the rich away empty.*
*He has helped his servant Israel,*
*in remembrance of his mercy,*
*according to the promise he*
*made to our ancestors,*
*to Abraham and to his*
*descendants forever.*

Luke: 1:47-55

Mary and Elizabeth were cousins.

tears, I was touched by the way God had worked in our lives. For years, people had been waiting for the Messiah—the one sent by God to save the world. It was finally coming true and I was a part of it.

I could not help but sing. The words just poured out of me. I was awestruck by the way God had chosen an ordinary person, me, to bear this special child. It could have been anyone. But that is how God works. God uses the most unknown—the lowly, the outcasts, the least of all the saints— to serve the needs of the world. The song I sang reflected a moment of truth in which I was filled with hope that justice would truly be served—the hungry would have enough food, the lowly would have a chance at life, and peace and love would rule the world.

Mary's song is also called "The Magnificat."

God truly does work in wonderful ways. One of the things I have learned is that God uses ordinary people and ordinary moments to tell about God's extraordinary promises. It is often in the everyday conversations between family members, neighbors, or coworkers that God's love is revealed. God promised the world a savior. The world would have thought this savior's mother would be a queen. But instead, God chose me. Wow! Who would have every thought that God's promises could happen like this! God truly is a God of mercy. I am deeply honored to bear God's son.

# John 11:17-27 Jesus: The Resurrection and the Life

**M**Y NAME IS MARTHA. My sister, Mary, my brother, Lazarus, and I live in Jerusalem. Not long ago, Lazarus got really sick. He had a high fever and ached all over. At first it seemed like just the seasonal flu. But when he kept getting worse, Mary and I called for Jesus. Jesus is a friend of our family. We knew that he could help us in a way that no one else could. But he did not come, at least not when we thought he should have.

Lazarus was barely breathing when the message came that Jesus would not be coming right away. I was really sad…and hurt…and even angry. I wanted Jesus to come. I knew he could make a difference. But all I could do was watch helplessly as my brother became more and more sick. His breathing was labored. Each breath he took was short and seemed as difficult for him as if he were trying to lift a cart full of bricks all by himself. It was very hard to watch him hurt so badly. It was very scary to know that he might die.

Mary and I sat beside him constantly. We put cool washcloths on his forehead, we sang his favorite songs, and we talked to him. We told him that we loved him and to hang in there because Jesus was coming…eventually.

I don't remember what time it was. It was dark, and still, and muggy hot. There were no stars in the sky. Dark clouds hid the light of the moon. Mary and I sat in the stillness of that night. The silence pounded our ears long after our brother had died.

The next few days were filled with preparation. We did all the things you have to do when a family member dies. And finally, we laid my brother to rest in a tomb at the edge of town.

**Being unresponsive** for four days was the criteria for declaring a person dead.

It was four days later—four days after my brother had died—that Jesus came. When he came, Jesus embraced me. I buried my face in his shoulder and sobbed. His hand smoothed my hair. His touch eased my trembling. When I had cried until I no longer had tears, I finally began to speak. I told him that I had hoped he could come sooner. He looked at me with his deep, compassionate eyes and said, "Martha, Martha. Your brother will rise again." He continued, "I am the resurrection and the life. Those who believe in me,

*"I am the resurrection and the life. Those who believe in me, even though they die, will live, and everyone who lives and believes in me will never die. Do you believe this?"*

John 11:25-26

even though they die, will live, and everyone who lives and believes in me will never die. Do you believe this?" (11:25-26).

I believed it with my whole heart. I answered, "Yes, Lord, I believe that you are the Messiah, the Son of God, the one coming into the world" (11:27).

I learned something new that day. Although Jesus raised my brother from the grave that very day, I learned that through Jesus Christ, God has promised that whether we live or whether we die, we are never beyond God's love, care, and power of restoration to new life. God's love in Jesus Christ breaks open the tombs. That which separates us from those we love is no more in Christ Jesus.

# Focus the Stories

*Grandpa's Problem*

"Grandpa, will you read this book to me?" asked the little boy as he climbed into his grandfather's lap. His grandfather responded, "Ah, no I can't right now, I need to take the dog for a walk—but maybe grandma could read it to you."

The little boy looked disappointed and said, "Grandpa, could you read it to me when you get back? This is my favorite book." "Maybe later," said the grandfather.

As he pulled on his coat, hat and gloves, and grabbed the dog's leash, he wondered why he had said, "maybe later." Later was not going to change anything. The fact of the matter was that he could not read at all—ever. Although he had been a highly successful carpenter during his working years, he had always relied on his wife to read whatever needed to be read. It is not that he didn't want to read—it was that he couldn't.

He remembered his teachers always telling him that he was stupid because he was never able to get the words right.

Not long ago, he wife had suggested that maybe he should take a class and try again. She thought maybe he had something called "dyslexia." It was possible that she was right. She explained that with the right teacher, maybe he could learn to read. As he headed home, he thought he might give it a try. Yet, what if he still couldn't learn? How would he ever be able to tell his grandson? He felt incredibly vulnerable.

*1.* Have you ever known a situation like the grandfather's? What did you do? How did you feel?

*2.* Knowing that women in Mary's time were punished for being pregnant outside of marriage, how might Mary, the mother of Jesus, have felt vulnerable?

*3.* When Martha has every reason to believe that Jesus has abandoned her and her family, he shows up on the scene. Have you ever had an experience when you thought God had abandoned you and later realized that it was not so?

*4.* Did God become vulnerable in the birth of Jesus? In the death of Jesus? Why or why not?

# ⑤ God Promises the Holy Spirit

*In order that we might know the fullness of God, God sends us the Holy Spirit.*

## John 14:15-17 Living with God's Spirit

MY NAME IS PHILIP. One day while I was in Galilee, Jesus invited me to be one of his disciples. Some friends from my hometown of Bethsaida, Andrew and Peter, had already become followers of Jesus. I decided to follow as well. After all, we had waited a long time to see the Messiah.

It was a privilege to travel with Jesus, to learn about God, to be a part of this world-changing event that was taking place in our midst. But every once in a while Jesus said something that was not easy to understand. Like the day when Jesus told us he was going away, we did not understand that he was going to be crucified and then rise again. Peter asked him where he was going. Jesus had responded by saying a peculiar thing. He said, "Where I am going, you cannot follow me now; but you will follow afterward" (John 13:36). Peter had pursued it further by asking why he could not follow right then. Jesus told Peter that eventually he would deny ever knowing Jesus. Peter really looked sad about that. I think that is why Thomas tried to clarify things a bit. Thomas asked, "Lord, we do not know where you are going. How can we know the way?" (14:5). Jesus had responded by saying that if we knew his Father, we would know the way. It was too confusing, like trying to find your way through the desert without a path. I tried. I asked him, "Lord, show us the Father, and we will be satisfied" (14:8). By then, I think Jesus was a little perturbed at our thick-headed ways. He answered,

"Have I been with you all this time, Philip, and you still do not know me?" (14:9). I felt terrible. Somehow, it seemed that I had offended this beloved friend. Of course I knew him—I had spent a lot of time with him.

I guess by then he figured that we needed to be told again. In his most compassionate way, he described himself in relation to God. He reminded us that not only was he our friend, our fellow human, but that he was also God's Son, and thereby an intimate part of God's very being. He told us that if we asked for something in his name, he would do whatever it was that we asked. Then he promised that he would send an Advocate to be with us forever. He said that the Advocate would be the Spirit of truth—God's spirit—that would actually live with us, just as Jesus did. We would not be alone.

Living with God's spirit is one of God's greatest blessings. Although it was really difficult to think about Jesus going away, having him promise that God's spirit would be with us reminded us all that God will never, ever abandon us or any of God's chosen children.

*Satisfy us in the morning*
*with your steadfast*
*love,*
*so that we may rejoice*
*and be glad all our*
*days.*
*Make us glad as many*
*days as you have*
*afflicted us,*
*and as many years as*
*we have seen evil.*
*Let your work be manifest*
*to your servants,*
*and your glorious*
*power to their*
*children.*
Psalm 90:14-16

M Y NAME IS PAUL. I wrote this letter to the people in Philippi while I was in prison. Because there were Jewish leaders who did not believe that Jesus was the Messiah, my preaching and teaching were not always welcome. In fact, sometimes it was dangerous to proclaim the good news of God in Jesus Christ. Yet, the people needed to hear. They needed to know what God has done for us, in us, and continues to do through us. They needed to know what happened the day Jesus died on the cross and the day he rose from the dead. They needed to know how God's spirit unites us as a community of faith.

So, I kept preaching and teaching until I was arrested and imprisoned. From prison, I wrote letters to the communities of faith through which I had traveled. The Letter of Paul to the Philippians was written to the people of Philippi. Some refer to this piece as a "love letter." I suppose they are right. I loved the people who shared my passion for the mission of the gospel.

I wrote this letter because I wanted the people of Philippi to know that I appreciated their sharing in the good news of Jesus Christ. I also wanted them to know that I was praying for them and that I hoped for their continued unity for the sake of the gospel.

It is not always easy to stay united. I asked that they would be of one mind—that they would try to think alike. It is so easy for hair-splitting disagreements to begin and thereby destroy the unity of

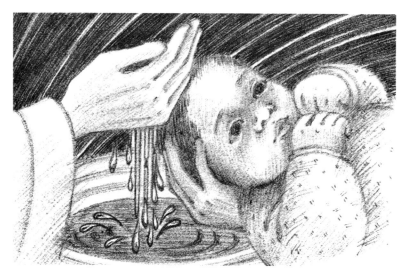

the community. My hope for them was that they would be able to put aside their differences and always focus on what they held in common. That, of course, was being united by the death and resurrection of Jesus Christ. Being baptized into life in Christ, being joined permanently as Christ's body in the world, I hoped that they would always be able to celebrate their oneness.

Because of that, I also asked them to live in love—the same love with which Christ has loved them. That kind of love, as I wrote in my first letter to the Corinthians, is patient and kind, not envious or boastful, not arrogant or rude. It does not insist on its own way, it is not irritable or resentful; it does not rejoice in wrongdoing, but rejoices in the truth. It bears all things, believes all things, hopes all things, and endures all things. That kind of love never ends (see 1 Corinthians 13:4-8).

Saul, who became Paul after encountering Christ on the road to Damascus, was blind for three days because of an intense light.

My prayer is that the people whom I love so much in Philippi know how Christ's death and resurrection is a promise. I pray they do not focus on the differences among them, but rather understand that what unites us is Christ Jesus. Our God has such a powerful and profound love for us. When we understand that, we begin to see and hear one another with new eyes and ears. For the promise is this: God is for us, and we know this through Jesus Christ and his death on the cross. Furthermore, God reveals all this to us through the Holy Spirit. We need not fear, God is with us always. And so we have hope and confidence, and we are given the "peace of God which passes all understanding." (Philippians 4:7).

# Focus the Stories

HAVE YOU EVER WONDERED how the Holy Spirit works in our lives? In his explanation of the Third Article of the Apostles' Creed, Martin Luther writes, "I believe that by my own understanding or strength I cannot believe in Jesus Christ my Lord or come to him, but instead the Holy Spirit has called me through the gospel, enlightened me with his gifts, made me holy, and kept me in the true faith, just as he calls, gathers, enlightens, and makes holy the whole Christian church on earth and keeps it with Jesus Christ in the one common, true faith." [1]

The writer of John's gospel tells us that though we cannot see the Holy Spirit, it will abide with us. The writer also tells us that the Holy Spirit is the Spirit of truth. Paul tells us in Philippians that the Holy Spirit brings peace and compassion for it unites us into Christ. Think for a moment about Luther's, Paul's and the gospel writer's words about the Holy Spirit. Now read the following vignettes and answer the questions that follow.

George (age 78): "Doctor, I know that my heart is not going to last forever. But you know, it's okay. I'm not afraid to die. Somehow, I have this sense of peace."

Liza (age 49): "You know, pastor, I was not going to come to church today—this week had been so hectic. But I decided I needed to come—and your sermon spoke right to me."

Mike (age 42): "It was fate. I knew that my son would make that basket to win the game."

*Questions*

**1.** Do you think that the Holy Spirit had anything to do with George's, Liza's or Mike's statements? Why or why not?

**2.** How does the explanation of Luther, Paul and John's gospel fit with your understanding of the Holy Spirit?

**3.** What do you think is the difference between fate and the work of the Holy Spirit?

**4.** Describe a situation when you believe the Holy Spirit was noticeably at work in your life.

1. From *A Contemporary Translation of Luther's Small Catechism* (Minneapolis: Augsburg Fortress © 1989), p. 23

# ⑥ God Promises a New Reality

Understanding God's faithfulness in the past,
we trust God's promise for the future

## Revelation 21:3b-4  Dwelling with God

IMAGINE A LIFE without tears, or fears, or death. Imagine a life without pain, without grief, without end. Throughout the generations, God has been faithful to God's people. In Jesus Christ, God has come to us, suffered with us, and has died and risen for us. By the power of the Holy Spirit, God has called us to be God's people and promised a future like none we have ever known before. Although we have not fully experienced this new reality, we can trust it to be true because God has promised that it will be true.

Revelation is not just the last book of the Bible. It also tells us the end of the story. It tells us that Jesus Christ will come again. Much of the imagery is strange and fantastic, but ultimately the message of Revelation is grounded in the same promise that weaves itself throughout the Bible. And this promise from God remains quite simple: *Do not fear, I will abide with you and protect you. You are safe, for I love you and will never forsake you.* God has promised that we will always be God's people.

It is difficult to imagine a life without tears, or fears, or death. But God is a faithful God. God keeps promises. God kept his promise to Abraham and Noah. God kept the promise of which the prophets spoke by sending a savior. God will keep the promises made to us.

# Focus the Story

*Jessie's Story*

SHE WAS ONLY SIX YEARS OLD. Yet, she had lived in and out of foster care most of her life. Although her mother tried, and meant to do well, she was not prepared to parent. On this first night in yet another foster home, Jessie was scared. As her foster mother was tucking her in, Jessie asked if she could look at her wedding ring. The foster mother, eager to comfort this little girl, slid the ring off her finger and let Jessie hold it. Jessie took the ring, and clamping it tightly, slid her little fist under the pillow. As she did that, she said, "There. Now you won't leave me while I sleep."

Fears, distrust, and anxieties caused by the broken nature of human relationships cause us to sometimes doubt the truth of God's promise to live with us forever. Yet, we have seen again and again throughout Israel's history that God is always faithful to promises. Even more, God made a promise to you in the cross and resurrection. Because of Christ, *nothing* can separate you from the love of God.

Image © Digital Stock Ccrp.

You see, when God makes a promise it is as sure and certain as the fact that water is part of the ocean. It is as sure and certain as the fact that Monday follows Sunday. It is as sure and certain as the fact that you were born. Make no mistake, God is always faithful to God's promises!

*See, the home of God is among mortals.*
*He will dwell with them as their God;*
*they will be his peoples,*
*and God himself will be with them;*
*he will wipe every tear from their eyes.*
*Death will be no more;*
*mourning and crying and pain will be no more,*
*for the first things have passed away.*

Revelation 21:3b-4